EVEN MORE
SURPRISE SKETCHES
Ronald Rich

Nimbus Press

COPYRIGHT

We are mainly interested in providing resources for churches that want to use drama in worship, in bible study and in evangelism, or for Amateur Dramatic groups. **You are free to perform any of our plays or sketches and do not need to ask for permission but we would be delighted to receive news of any productions. All our plays and sketches are protected by copyright and so we ask that you buy copies for each actor when you perform one.** We hope that you will find them useful for the work of the Kingdom.

Fees for performances by professional companies will be subject to negotiation.

This edition 1999 Nimbus Press,
18 Guilford Road, Leicester, LE2 2RB

First published in 1998

Copyright © Ronald Rich 1998

British Library Cataloguing in Publication
Data available

ISBN 1 874424 42 X

Printed in Great Britain by
Moorleys Print & Publishing, Ilkeston, Derbys.

Contents

Note. *The sex of the characters listed below is not always as specified in the sketches but where they are listed as 'm. or f.' this means that they could be changed without any difficulty.*

Page

VIEW FROM THE HILL   5
2 m., 2 f.   Consideration of our stewardship of the earth and thankfulness to God for the wonder of His creation.

BEDSIDE MANNA   13
2 m. or f.   We may become aware of God even though there is pain and suffering in the world.

ARE YOU SITTING COMFORTABLY?   15
4 m. or f.   The full implications of belonging to the church.

YOU AND ME BOTH   20
3 m. or f.   Do not judge people by outward appearance or put 'labels' on them.

MEET THE BOSS   23
6 m. or f.   Are we honest with ourselves about our own characters?

CAN YOU SPARE A MINUTE?   28
1m., 1f.   Good things may happen if we really get to know other people.

IN TOUCH   35
2m., 2f.   Inconsistent behaviour of those who don't like to 'pass the peace'.

STAR STRUCK   36
2f.   The folly of belief in astrology.

CALLED TO PREACH   40
2m. or f.   Do we fail to 'communicate'?

CAUGHT IN THE NET   42
1m., 1f.   The dangers of being too absorbed in our own concerns or interests.

Introduction

Ronald Rich's previous two books of short dramatic pieces *(Surprise Sketches* and *More Surprise Sketches)* were eagerly used by Church drama groups and sold in the thousands. We are pleased that this new collection is so popular and that we are already able to offer this new edition.

The Gospels know all about getting across Christian themes by means of stories or parables. These short sketches also seek to introduce Christian themes in a way that will capture the imagination and stay in the mind.

How well do we know each other? How good are we at listening? Has God really put the world into our keeping? How committed is our Church membership?

All are written for between two and five people, are suitable for use during worship services, and require few or no props.

Ten sketches to raise a smile and make you think.

THE VIEW FROM THE HILL

Characters: ADAM and EVE.
                  ADAM 2 and EVELYN.

A young man and woman are seen on a raised mound. EVE is sitting. ADAM, also in view, comes from back R. to stand near her. EVE is dressed in a body stocking or leotard. Both have suitably entwined leaves.

ADAM	That's it then, Eve. *(He looks round on the scene)*
EVE	Oh, Adam! Couldn't you have done something?
ADAM	*(Irked)* Done something! Like what?
EVE	You should have asserted yourself.
ADAM	But that's what started it all! I shouldn't have listened to you, that's what I *should* have done.
EVE	Well, anyway, here we are - outside. What are we going to do?
ADAM	Give me time - let me think. We were given some instructions, but it was all so traumatic. I'm not sure I remember them.
EVE	There weren't that many.
ADAM	I tell you I was shocked, dazed. Couldn't take it all in.
EVE	Will we ever get back?
ADAM	To the garden? Who knows?
EVE	*(EVE looks round her and makes a sweeping gesture with her arms)* Then we'll just have to make all this into a garden.
ADAM	You've got more imagination than I have.
EVE	But it's beautiful - in a rugged sort of way.
ADAM	Never mind about gardens. We have to survive. We must find out who our enemies are.
EVE	*(Puzzled)* Enemies?
ADAM	Some of these animals *(Points L.)* look as though they could eat us, for a start.
EVE	*(Deeply shocked)* They wouldn't!
ADAM	Oh, wouldn't they? I expect they're asking the same question as we are: 'how do we survive'? *(Pause)* And then we must find out what we can eat.
EVE	And what we shouldn't eat.
ADAM	I don't think you'd better mention that!

EVE	There's so much we ought to know. How do we find out about all this? *(She indicates the landscape)*
ADAM	Leave it to me, Eve. I'll fathom it out.
EVE	We could ask.
ADAM	*(Sharply)* No, we can't. Not out here. There's no-one to ask out here.
EVE	Why are you so sure of yourself?
ADAM	*(Taps his forehead)* Because of this, Eve. I can think. I tell you, we'll work it out. *(Suddenly)* I've just remembered ...!
EVE	*(Also remembering)* Work!
ADAM	Yes! We have to till the soil and tend the crops and work by the sweat of our brow.
EVE	Well, I don't mind.
ADAM	Good! You can start.
EVE	I already have. I found the way to stitch leaves together. *(She fingers the leaves around her waist)* I shall be able to make a shelter from the rain and the sun.
ADAM	Right. And I shall go out and kill something.
EVE	*(Shocked)* Kill something?
ADAM	Something to eat. A bear, an ox, or maybe a deer.
EVE	You weren't listening. I knew you weren't listening. We are to eat growing things, berries, fruits, corn.
ADAM	*(Patiently)* That was in there. We make our own rules out here.
EVE	But if we start killing each other, where will it end?
ADAM	We have to survive, Eve. Rule number one - eat or be eaten. Now you get busy making your shelter. I'll go off and find some food. *(He begins to go off R.)*
EVE	Green and growing, Adam.
ADAM	*(He pauses)* It's all down to us, isn't it? Just us.
EVE	We've got each other, Adam.
ADAM	*(With dawning realisation of power)* We can do anything we want.
EVE	A garden of our own.

ADAM goes to EVE and takes her by the shoulders.

ADAM	*(Admiringly)* I think I've picked the right help-meet, Eve.
EVE	*(Smiling)* Well, it wasn't difficult, was it?

They both laugh. ADAM goes off R. EVE moves to a lower spot off the mound summit R., and begins to experiment with entwining leaves. She remains in view, but becomes quite still.

~~~~~~~~~~~~~~~~~~~

Two modern young people enter from R. They are ADAM 2 and EVELYN. ADAM 2 is dressed in casual clothes and may have on trainers, but EVELYN is wearing a dress and more formal shoes. Though EVE remains in view they do not see her even when looking in her direction. EVELYN arrives CENTRE. She is exhilarated by the walk up the hill.

EVELYN   Come on, Adam. *(He follows immediately. They both look round them.)* I used to come here as a child with my parents. You can see for miles. *(She points downhill L.)* Look, there's the church. *(Pause)* You can really breathe up here. *(She breathes deeply)* It makes me want to dance. *(EVELYN does a 'twirl' or two)*

ADAM   Well, don't breathe too deeply, Evelyn.

EVELYN   It does you good.

ADAM   I read in the paper - yesterday - something to do with those factories in the estuary, and the power station. When the wind direction and humidity are both right, it's lethal up here.

EVELYN   *(Surprised)* Up here? Surely not. It's so beautiful.

ADAM   Nowhere's safe these days. *(Pause)* The policemen in Tokyo wear gas masks on traffic duty, you know. *(EVELYN laughs. ADAM 2 laughs with her.)* It's true!

EVELYN   My Dad always says to enjoy all this while you can, because it won't last.

ADAM   The view?

EVELYN   Yes. He says an area of countryside the size of the Isle of Wight goes under concrete in Britain every year.

ADAM   Not many people know that!

EVELYN   Are you 'green' Adam?

ADAM   *(Gets close to her)* That depends.

EVELYN   I am. *(She takes a step away)* You have to be. We could spoil it all. Did you know that ...

ADAM   Here we go!

EVELYN   ... did you know that most of the world's deserts are man-made? Greedy people who uprooted forests till all that was left was dust and nature just couldn't recover from it.

ADAM   They're still doing it in the rain forests, aren't they?

EVELYN   It's madness. *(Pause)* I want to be able to bring my children up here. To enjoy what I enjoy.

ADAM   We shall, Evelyn.

EVELYN   *(She gets the point, and smiles at him.)* I wonder. All the pollution, the dirty rivers, the nuclear waste ...

ADAM   ... pesticides, motorways ...

EVELYN   Can we sort it all out in time?

ADAM   *(Confidently)* Don't worry, they will.

EVELYN   They? And who might they be?

ADAM 2 and EVELYN turn to look off L. and remain still.

~~~~~~~~~~~~~~~~~~

ADAM returns from R. He is carrying a collection of assorted fruits and vegetables.

ADAM   Can you do anything with all this?

EVE   *(EVE takes some of the fruit.)* These look lovely.

ADAM   I'm hungry. I could eat a horse.

EVE   *(Reprovingly)* Adam!

ADAM   *(ADAM holds up some fruit, reluctantly agreeing)* This will be fine.

They both eat for a moment. EVE stops.

EVE   We shan't always be alone, shall we Adam? *(ADAM goes on eating.)* I mean - the garden we're making. I want to show it to them. *(ADAM still eats.)*

ADAM   Them?

EVE   Our children, Adam. I want them to be proud of what we've done.

ADAM   They will, Eve. They will.

EVE walks higher on the mound. She becomes animated.

8.

EVE   I want to bring them to this spot and say 'this is what we have done. And we've done it for you'. Well, we've made a start. Oh, Adam don't you feel thankful?

ADAM finishes eating and wipes his lips.

ADAM   *(Casually)* Of course I do.

EVE turns to him.

EVE   *(Makes a sudden decision)* I think we should say so.
ADAM   I did! I *am* thankful, Eve.
EVE   No. I mean we should tell someone.
ADAM   I don't know what you mean. There's no-one to tell, Eve. No-one to thank. We've done it all ourselves. You've earned it, Eve. Remember that. *(He waves an arm)* All this is yours.
EVE   Wasn't it here already.
ADAM   We've made it better. We don't owe anyone anything.

Pause.

EVE   *(Slowly)* This morning when I walked out, I saw the sun rise and all the forest was shot through with gold. The air was filled with the sound of bird song. I looked back at our little home and I knew you were there - my heart was ready to burst. I just wanted to hug someone and say - 'Thank you!'

ADAM goes to her.

     Don't you feel like that?
ADAM   I'll say this much. There are so many good things to eat. So many fish in the rivers, so much abundance in the forest. So much beauty in the mountains and in the flight of birds - yes - I have felt that someone was on my side, wanting me to survive. To live. To enjoy it all.
EVE   Then let's say 'Thank you'.
ADAM   *(Gruffly)* No!
EVE   Adam!

9.

They turn half R. and remain still.

~~~~~~~~~~~~~~~~~~~~

ADAM 2 and EVELYN turn to face forward. A sound of church bells is heard in the distance. EVELYN looks at her watch.

ADAM   I could stay here for ever.

EVELYN   It takes twenty minutes to reach the church from here. Come on!

ADAM   Look, Evelyn, I'll come as far as the village, but I'm not coming in - to the service I mean. You know how I feel about all that.

EVELYN   I know.

ADAM   Can't we stay up here for once? I mean it's all God's world, isn't it?

EVELYN   What do you think, Adam?

ADAM   *(Lightly)* Oh, yes. He made it I suppose.

EVELYN   He did more than that.

ADAM   More? Like what?

EVELYN   You know, 'God so loved the world ... '

ADAM   Oh, yes ... well, that too, I suppose. Look - if it's God's world, then it's God's world up here. We can thank him where we are.

EVELYN   *(Facing him)* But you won't, will you?

ADAM   Well, you know what I mean.

EVELYN   *(Decisively)* I'm going down, Adam. *(She moves L.)*

ADAM   Evelyn.

EVELYN   Are you coming?

ADAM   *(Warning)* But I'm not coming in.

EVELYN stops.

EVELYN   What are you so frightened of?

ADAM   Frightened - me? Huh! Frightened of what?

They 'freeze'.

~~~~~~~~~~~~~~~~~~~~

ADAM goes to eat another apple. EVE takes it gently but firmly from him.

EVE But I *want* to say it, Adam. I need to say it. Can't you understand that?
ADAM I told you, Eve. All this is ours. You owe nothing.
EVE What are you so frightened of?
ADAM Frightened? Is that what you think?
EVE You have a short memory, Adam. In the garden back there.
ADAM All right, all right. Yes, I was frightened. I was - in there.
EVE You hid yourself.
ADAM I know!! I know. But out here ... it's different. This is ours, Eve. Ours. *(Touch of uncertainty creeps in)* Isn't it?

They search each others eyes for some certainty. They freeze'.

~~~~~~~~~~~~~~~~~~

ADAM 2 and EVELYN face each other.

EVELYN Well - since you ask me - I'll tell you. You're frightened of saying 'Thank you', that's what. Frightened of admitting you need to.
ADAM That's ridiculous.
EVELYN Is it?
ADAM *(Giving in)* All right. How's this?

He stands off a little forward of EVELYN and spreads his arms. He calls out with increasing loudness.

Thank you! Thank you!! THANK YOU!!

EVELYN reproves him with mock sternness. He goes back to her and looks directly at her.

(Quietly) I do mean it, Evelyn.

EVELYN takes the initiative and embraces ADAM 2. They then stand with arms round each other's waist looking off L.

11.

~~~~~~~~~~~~~~~~~~~~

ADAM and EVE, from facing each other, now turn to the front.

ADAM   All right. *(Pause)* Well, you start.

Pause.

EVE   *(Hesitantly)* For giving us all this ... *(She makes a sweeping gesture with her arm)*

ADAM   *(Gently)* Go on.

EVE   ... for trusting us with it all. *(EVE looks to ADAM.)*

ADAM   For this wonderful world.

EVE   For this - garden.

ADAM   For ... all that's good around us ... *(He looks at EVE.)* ... and close to us.

EVE   Thank you! *(Ecstatically)* Oh, thank you!

Pause.

ADAM   *(Quietly)* Thank you.

Longer pause.

(Looking outward) Do you think anyone heard?

They all hold their positions. We hear again, faintly, the distant church bells. The light on stage perceptibly brightens, holds for a moment. They walk off stage, ADAM and EVE to the R., and ADAM 2 and EVELYN to the L.

END

BEDSIDE MANNA

Characters: BILL   A patient.
                PADRE   The hospital chaplain.

A patient in hospital is visited by the hospital chaplain.

PADRE   Hallo, how are you? Bill, isn't it?

BILL   That's right. Not too bad. Improving, so they say.

PADRE   That's good.

BILL   Who sent you then? I'm not one of your flock.

PADRE   I'm the hospital chaplain.

BILL   Oh, right. But I might as well come clean - I don't go to church. In fact, to be honest, I don't believe in God at all. Sorry padre but there you are. No offence, but I just can't see it.

PADRE   Maybe I can help.

BILL   *(Dismissive)* I mean, he's done nothing for me for a start, has he?

PADRE   God?

BILL   Yes.

PADRE   But you said he doesn't exist.

BILL   Well, I mean, look all round you.

PADRE   *(Looks)* I see a lot of people being well looked after, Bill, twenty four hours a day in a wonderful hospital.

BILL   *(Concedes)* Oh, yes. Great place. *(Triumphantly)* But they shouldn't be here at all, should they? I mean, if God took a walk through here - one word from him and we'd all be on our bikes. But he lets it happen, doesn't he?

PADRE   Who does?

BILL   God, of course!

PADRE   But didn't you say ...?

BILL   You know what I mean. It shouldn't happen, should it, not if him up there was keeping tabs? No, Vicar, sorry, you're on a loser there. I've worked it out for myself. I've nothing against you folk. You're all right, but when you look round you - you know, floods, earthquakes, HIV, loads of things - why even the Pope's got rheumatism! And if *he* can't get looked after, there's not much chance for you and me, eh? Doesn't add up, does it? Now, if I had his power ...

PADRE   What power is that, Bill?

BILL	Well, as I understand it, correct me if I'm wrong, he can do anything. Anything he wants, right?
PADRE	That's right.
BILL	So why doesn't he do it?
PADRE	He does, Bill. Look at all this. *(Waves his arm)*
BILL	But they shouldn't be here in the first place.
PADRE	You mean it would be nice to have a world where nothing ever went wrong, where you can't fall ill. No danger, no surprises, no problems.
BILL	Sounds all right to me.
PADRE	Where you can fall down stairs *(Points)* like that chap in the next bed, but never break any bones.
BILL	Save a lot of trouble, wouldn't it?
PADRE	Oh, yes. Solve everything. That is if you want a world of robots.
BILL	Well, as long as he knows what's going on, that's all. *(More solemn)* Life's pretty rotten for a lot of people, you know.
PADRE	He knows all about that, Bill.
BILL	*(Sceptical)* Oh?
PADRE	He's been right here with us and suffered quite a bit himself.
BILL	*(Softening a little)* Look, Padre, I'm not blaming you. Nothing personal. But he's got his work cut out to convince me, that's all. I like to say what I mean.
PADRE	So you should, Bill. Why don't you tell him?
BILL	*(Surprised)* Tell him? I don't think he'd like that.
PADRE	Oh, he would Bill, I promise you.
BILL	That is, if he exists, of course.
PADRE	Of course.
BILL	Otherwise I'm talking to myself, eh? *(Laughs)*
PADRE	*(Gently, very serious)* Are you, Bill?
BILL	*(Pause)* Maybe not.

The Chaplain extends his hand, which Bill shakes warmly.

Thanks.

END

ARE YOU SITTING COMFORTABLY?

Four characters (A,B,C,D) male or female, any age. They enter,talking.

C	But what exactly do you mean by 'membership'?
A	Well, its about belonging to something, isn't it?
C	What, like the Co-op?
A	*(Disgusted)* No!
C	Aston Villa?
A	Can we be serious for a minute?
C	I'm only asking. You said ...
A	As I understand it, it's about belonging not to some*thing* - but to some*one*. It's about following someone.
C	What, anyone? A pop star?
A	Of course not!
C	Why not? Lots of young people do.
A	They're just admirers. I'm talking about followers, a way of life. Its really all about total commitment.
B	I know a story about that.
C	*(Wearily)* Some other time
A	*(Encouraging)* No, go on. What story?
C	Don't encourage him.
A	Shall we sit down?

They sit. B remains standing.

B   Well, it was during the war. A small group of Jews were in the same hut in a Nazi concentration camp. They shared their faith and became close friends. One of them was a servant to the camp guards and he managed to get hold of two lumps of sugar. He brought them back to the hut and showed them to his friends. They all envied him. They hadn't seen sugar for years. They congratulated him. But at the end of the day in his bunk, the lucky owner of the sugar couldn't bring himself to eat it. He kept thinking of his friends. So next day, secretly, he gave the sugar lumps to one of them telling him to enjoy them and to say nothing about the gift. He thought no more about it. Years later at the end of the war the camp was liberated and they were free. After some years they met. While they celebrated together, one of them said: I've got something to show you. Something I always look at and think of you, my dearest friends. And he brought out the now dusty sugar lumps. They all smiled. It transpired that while in the concentration camp the sugar had been passed round gradually to all of them in turn, every time in secret without the others knowing. No-one had felt able to eat them. Each had passed them on to someone else. Despite their emaciated skeleton frames and desperate hunger they couldn't enjoy that luxury by themselves. The sugar lumps were kept as a reminder of their love for each other.

D   That's a good story. Commitment to each other. Because of what they had shared together.

B   That's right. And it really happened.

C   Well I've got a story too. Do you want to hear it?

A   Why not?

C   This is true as well. I know an old lady who lives alone. The one bright spot in her week was going to the church and to the Women's Meeting. Done it for donkey's years. Then she fell ill, and the ambulance took her off to hospital with a welfare officer. At the hospital the Ward Sister looked at this poor old soul who clearly had precious little money and was old enough to have outlived all her friends. Do you live alone, asked the Ward Sister? Yes, she does, said the social worker, answering for the old lady who looked too tired and unwell to reply. Has she any relatives? No, said the Social Worker. The Sister then wrote a note in her record and said it out loud as she wrote. 'No family'. The old lady stirred herself at this and looked indignantly at the Ward Sister. 'What did you say?' 'You have no family, have you?' repeated the Ward Sister, kindly. The old lady raised herself up. 'No family?' she said. 'I've got hundreds of them!' The Ward Sister looked a bit surprised but it was true. The old lady was thinking of her church and all those folk she worshipped with week by week, and the Women's Meeting where she was so well known and loved and missed. 'Family?' she said, 'I've got hundreds of them.'

D   I like that. A lovely story. They were committed to each other and they made sure the old lady never felt alone.

A	O.K., so are we saying being a Christian is being committed and having great fellowship with others who are committed too. You belong to them in a special way because you all belong to the same Master.
C	Well, that's it then, isn't it? Problem solved. *(Stands)*
D	I think we're getting somewhere. But I don't think we have *quite* got there yet.

C sits again. A coughs loudly

D	Something tells me you have story too.
A	As it happens, yes. *(Proudly)* My story is in the Bible.
B/C	*(Teasing)* Whooo!
D	So, what's your story?
A	David and his bodyguard were at war with with the Philistines and they were hiding in a cave - David and his men, that is. They were safe as long as they stayed there, but the trouble was they had no water. You can live without food for quite a long time, but you must have water. And the only water within distance was at a nearby well ...
B	No problem.
A	Big problem! The well happened to be by the the gates of Bethlehem which was fortified and held by the Philistine army. It would be suicide to try and get it. But they remembered what David said. They *must* have water if they were to carry on. Without another word three of his men left the cave and managed to get through the Philistine lines and brought up water from the well which they brought back to David in the cave. When they gave it proudly to David, he was so touched by what they had done that he couldn't drink it, but poured it out on the ground saying it was too precious to drink, having been brought at the risk of his men's lives.
B	Because they'd risked everything for him.
A	Yes, it made them a band of brothers.
C	Committed to each other.
D	That's great, but I don't think it takes us all the way. It's time to say just where our commitment really starts.
B	Do I sense another story? *(Smiles from the rest)*

D	Why not? There was this group of friends who set out on a quest to look for the one who knew more than anyone else about what it means to be human. They were not looking for the *cleverest* man in the world. Not the most *powerful*. Not the most *successful*, even. But simply the *best*. They looked everywhere, but everybody, however good they sounded, however persuasive, was flawed. But they didn't give up. They knew they would find him in the end. Then one of them asked the others: what will you do when you find him? The first one answered 'I shall say to him: I have come to serve you. And then I shall stretch out my hands and offer him my gifts.' Another one replied: 'I shall say to him I have come to learn. And I shall look up to him for wisdom and advice.' The third one then said, 'I shall say to him: I have come to worship. And I shall kneel before him and praise him.' The three then looked at the fourth friend and they asked, what about you? The fourth man answered: I shall say to him, ' I heard you call my name. I came because I had to. I put my life in your hands.'
B	O.K. That's it, then. End of story.
D	Wrong. Beginning of story.
A	What?
D	Don't you recognise those people?
C	No. Should we?
D	Those four people are us.
A	Whoa! Hang on. I've been a member of the Church since I was about three.
B	And I was made a member with a whole group of us from the Youth Club when I was fourteen.
C	Well, I'm not actually a member *as such*, but I'm in my place most Sundays, *(Proudly)* and I do have a book of offertory envelopes.
A	Greater love hath no man!
D	You all sound very pleased about it. So, let me ask you: are you saying you've found the right man?
A	'Course }
B	Oh, yes } Together
C	No doubt in my mind }
A	None at all. }
D	There's one thing left to do, then.
B	Commitment?

D	That's right.
C	Bit late for that isn't it? I mean ...
D	Is it?

Pause.

A	*(Awkwardly)* Well - I'll just slip back into my seat, if that's O.K with you. *(Sits with audience)*
B	Good idea, I'll join you. *(Does the same)*
C	Wait for me. *(Calls back as he goes)* Good sketch. *(Sits with audience)*
D	*(Speaks to them now in the audience)* You can't hide there. I forgot to tell you the last bit of the story. *He's* looking for *you.* And his commitment to *that* is total.

D exits.

END

YOU AND ME, BOTH

Characters: THEATRE DIRECTOR
               PARSON
               TEENAGER

Two people are on stage sitting next to each other looking straight ahead. One is a TEENAGER, the other is an older, but not old, man. The TEENAGER is dressed in high punk style: jeans, leathers, chains, bovver boots, a ring in the ear or nose, and appropriate hairstyle. Beside him is a ghetto-blaster. The man is a PARSON and is neatly dressed and wears a clerical collar. The PARSON looks furtively at the TEENAGER and registers curiosity and some amazement. The TEENAGER looks ahead. The TEENAGER then steals a glance at the PARSON and promptly angles himself slightly in the other direction. A woman hurries in carrying a clipboard and papers. She is a DIRECTOR.

DIR.   Sorry to keep you waiting. I'm the Director.

They both stand briefly.

It's all go, I'm afraid. You've both come to audition for a part in the play. Good. *(Looks slightly uncertainly at them)* H'm. Fascinating. I must hear you read, of course. Just relax.

She lifts out a sheet of paper.

(To TEENAGER) Perhaps you could start.

She hands him the sheet of paper.

In your own time.

She retires to edge of the stage. The TEENAGER looks at the sheet of paper for a moment then briefly looks at the PARSON and back to the paper. He coughs then begins to read, slowly at first, then gaining confidence.

TEEN.   I'm quite aware that my appearance probably causes you problems. But I happen to like dressing this way. At least you know who I am. And I certainly don't want to look like you. *(He looks briefly at the PARSON and then at the DIRECTOR)*

DIR.   That's fine. Carry on.

TEEN.   My own sort accept me, that's what matters. Come to think of it we haven't got much in common. You hate my music and just don't understand it. You don't approve of the language I use. If the truth's known you probably don't understand it either. Still, I don't suppose you could help becoming what you are. It was predictable wasn't it? You just accepted it. That's water under the bridge now. I expect you took one look at me and thought 'How did he get like that? I bet he's got a one-track mind. He's not a normal person like me.' But how do you know? If we ever *do* meet - properly I mean - I expect you'll find out I'm really O.K. but you won't take that chance, will you? What a pity. *(He looks up)*

DIR.   Right, thank you.

She holds out her hand for the script and takes it from the TEENAGER. She puts it with other sheets on her clipboard and makes a brief note.

Now! *(To PARSON)* Will you read for me?

She hands him the script.

In your own time.

The PARSON gives a brief not unfriendly glance to the TEENAGER, then begins to read.

PARSON   I'm quite aware that my appearance probably causes you problems. But I happen to like dressing - this way. *(He fingers his collar)* At least you know who I am. And I certainly don't want to look like *you.*

TEENAGER *looks down at his own clothes. He raises his eyebrows and is clearly not displeased with what he sees.*

My own sort accept me, that's what matters. Come to think of it we haven't got much in common. You hate my music and just don't understand it. You don't approve of the language I use. If the truth's known you probably don't understand it either. Still, I don't suppose you could help becoming what you are. It was predictable wasn't it? You just accepted it. That's water under the bridge now. I expect you took one look at me and thought 'How did he get like that'. And, 'I bet he's got a one-track mind. He's not a normal person like me.' But how do you know? If we ever *do* meet - properly I mean - I expect you'll find out I'm really O.K. but you won't take that chance, will you? What a pity.

DIR.   *(Intervenes)* O.K. Great, thank you.

She takes back the script.

Excellent. *(To both)* I can see you've done this before. I'll make up my mind and let you know. You can get some coffee over there. *(Points off)* Thank you very much. I'll be in touch.

She exits. The TEENAGER and PARSON look at each other. Pause.

PARSON   You were very good.
TEEN.   Nah! You were OK though. *(Holds out his hand)* I'm Winston.
PARSON   *(Shakes his hand)* I'm the Revd ... *(Changes his mind)* I'm John. Fancy a coffee?
TEEN.   Why not?

They begin to walk off, talking.

PARSON   Doesn't that ring in your nose hurt?
TEEN.   No more than your collar.

They laugh. When almost off, the TEENAGER turns on his ghetto-blaster. The PARSON smiles and puts his hands over his ears as they ... EXIT.
                              END

MEET THE BOSS

Characters: COOPER   ) Candidates
               TURNER   ) for a job
               FOSTER   ) interview.
               BEST   )
               READER   Quiet, in corner.
               MAN   Candidate who arrives later.

A group of people sit in what seems to be a waiting room. There are more chairs than people and no-one sits alongside anyone else. One man, TURNER, is restless and he fidgets with his tie, his breast pocket handkerchief, his cuffs. He rubs his shoes against his trousers to polish them. A woman, FOSTER, sits upright keeping herself to herself. A third man sits quietly reading. A fourth person, COOPER, is jovial and untroubled. A second woman, BEST, is three seats from anyone else.

COOPER   *(To TURNER)* You been here long?
TURNER   Not really.
COOPER   Seems long though, doesn't it?
TURNER   Yes, it does. Seems a long time. *(Nods towards door)* Is someone in there with him now?
COOPER   I expect so

          Pause.

TURNER   You realise we are all after the same position?
COOPER   Well, may the best man win.
FOSTER   Or woman, as the case may be.
COOPER   Oh, yes. Sorry.
TURNER   This is important to me. I really want this, you know.
FOSTER   You'll have to prove yourself, like the rest of us.
BEST   *(Loftily)* I don't want to depress you, but I think you may all be wasting your time.
COOPER   Oh, yes? What makes you think that? Are you a relative of his or something?
BEST   Not exactly. *(Smugly)* But I can claim, shall we say, some acquaintance.

23.

TURNER *(Upset)* Well, that's it then! *(He stands up)* It's all a set up. All this is just the appearance of fairness. It's already been decided beforehand, has it? Might as well go home.

COOPER Sit down!

TURNER sits.

BEST No, its all above board, but the truth is I am particularly well qualified. That's what counts after all.

COOPER So *you* say.

FOSTER I think it's all a matter of presenting yourself properly.

TURNER *(Sarcastically)* You mean telling lies about yourself.

FOSTER Of course not! Well ... not actual *lies* but ...

TURNER But it's true, isn't it? I mean, you don't go in and say 'I'm not very good' You say 'I'm first class. Top drawer. Just the sort of person you're looking for'. You've got to sell yourself. Go over the top a bit. Its all in the game.

BEST A good boss can spot *real* quality a mile off.

COOPER Like you, eh? *(Snorts)*

Pause.

FOSTER *(Vehemently)* I *need* this position. Its not an extra for me, it's essential.

BEST That cuts no ice. Sentiment doesn't come into it. Can you cut the mustard, that's what matters. *(Pause)* Have you got a decent reference?

FOSTER Oh, yes. *(Taps handbag)* It even makes me blush.

TURNER Lucky you. That good, is it?

BEST Ah, but it all depends who wrote it. Anyone of substance?

FOSTER I wrote it myself. *(Interrupts gasps of horror)* Well - in a way. It's not what you think. I just put down all the good points I didn't want him to miss.

TURNER But that's terrible! I've got a good mind to ...

FOSTER Don't you dare. Its all in the game. Didn't you just say that?

TURNER *(Gives in)* All right. All right. *(Pause)* I just wish he'd get a move on. This waiting is making me nervous.

Pause.

24.

FOSTER   What will you do if you're turned down?
TURNER   Me? I don't know, I don't like to think about it.
FOSTER   *(To COOPER)* You?
COOPER   *(Casually)* I'm not bothered to be honest. I'll think of something else.
TURNER   *(To BEST)* No point in asking you, is there?

BEST just smiles. Pause.

TURNER   *(Looking at door)* Come *on.* Come *on!*
COOPER   What about him over there? *(Nods towards the fifth person who is still reading)*
TURNER   I don't know. Ask him. *(Pause)* Go on!
COOPER   *(To READER)* Excuse me.

READER looks up.

COOPER   You're very quiet. You waiting to see the boss?
READER   No.
COOPER   *(Satisfied)* Oh, good. *(To TURNER)* He's not waiting to see the boss.
READER   *(Closes his book)* I *am* the boss.

General surprise, anguish. Cries of 'But', 'Never', 'You?', 'What?'

FOSTER   Then what are you doing here?
READER   I find I learn so much more by being out here among the people. Its very instructive.
TURNER   *(Horrified)* Then you must have heard ...?
READER   Oh, yes. I heard everything.
FOSTER   But that's not fair.
READER   Isn't it?
COOPER   We thought ...
READER   You thought I was in there, out of sight, behind closed doors. You thought that you could ignore me till the moment came, then you would come in and *(Looks at BEST)* dazzle me with your brilliance, *(Looks at COOPER)* disguise your insincerity, *(Looks at FOSTER)* and mislead me with your lies.
COOPER   That's it, then. We've blown it.

BEST stands.

BEST   *(Pompously)* I think I would like to make a statement.
FOSTER   Oh, shut up!
READER   *(Smiling)* I think you've all got some thinking to do.
COOPER   Does that mean ...?
READER   My door is always open. If you really mean business, you'll make it.
TURNER   Well, thank you. *(Beams with gratitude)* After all you're the boss.

The READER smiles. They gradually exit talking as they go.

FOSTER   That's very fair.
TURNER   I agree ...
BEST   But my suitability stands out a mile. I thought he might have noticed.
COOPER   What about me ...?

They all exit. READER resumes his seat and opens his book and begins to read. A MAN comes in and hesitantly looks round, observes the READER, and sits down.

Pause.

MAN   Am I too late?

READER looks up.

READER   Oh, no.

The MAN now comes closer and chooses a seat just two away from the READER.

MAN   Nervous? So am I. Look, don't worry. Just be totally honest. It pays in the end, believe me. *(Taps him on the knee)* You'll be all right, you see.
READER   You sound as though you want me to succeed.
MAN   *(Surprised)* Of course. Why not? We all want that, don't we?

26.

READER simply smiles. After a moment the MAN walks over to the door R.

MAN   *(Looking at the door)* I wonder what he's really like?

The READER gets up and goes to MAN.

READER   Shall we come and see?

READER motions with his arm for the MAN to go forward.

MAN   If he takes me, he'll take anybody.
READER   I think you'll do just fine.

MAN exits R., READER follows.

END

CAN YOU SPARE A MINUTE?

Characters: WOMAN   Market researcher.
                 MAN   Being interviewed.

A woman in her thirties dressed in outdoor clothes is on stage. She carries a handbag over her shoulder and wields a pencil and a clipboard. She has the predatory manner of the market researcher. A MAN enters R. His age is around forty.

WOMAN   Excuse me, could you spare a minute?
MAN   *(Taken by surprise)* What!
WOMAN   We are doing some market research. Could you answer a few simple questions?
MAN   *(Not very willing)* No, I don't think ...
WOMAN   Its about social habits.
MAN   *(Almost relenting)* I don't know.
WOMAN   It won't take a minute. *(Engagingly)* Please?

He shrugs. She consults her notes.

Are you married ... widowed ... single ...?
MAN   Divorced.
WOMAN   *(She makes a note)* Right. Do you live alone? I mean, your children don't live with you?
MAN   No. No children.
WOMAN   Rather boring list coming up.

She reels off her questions without looking up making a note as each answer is given.

WOMAN   You have a television?
MAN   Of course.
WOMAN   Video?
MAN   Yes.
WOMAN   C.D. player?
MAN   Yes.
WOMAN   Microwave?

MAN   Not now.

WOMAN looks up, briefly.

She took that.
WOMAN   Dishwasher?
MAN   *And* that.
WOMAN   Do you have a car - or two?
MAN   One car.
WOMAN   Do you travel abroad for your holidays?
MAN   Look, is all this getting anywhere?

WOMAN looks up.

WOMAN   Oh, you'd be surprised how important it is. Do you take a weekly magazine?
MAN   No.
WOMAN   Do you take one, or two, daily papers?
MAN   None.
WOMAN   *(She eyes him sharply)* None! Now that *is* surprising. Is it a life-long habit, or some conviction about the Press?
MAN   Nothing like that. I cancelled the papers only yesterday.
WOMAN   Cancelled?
MAN   Yes.
WOMAN   You mean ...?
MAN   Permanently.
WOMAN   *(Puzzled)* Oh.
MAN   I don't need them. *(Pause)* Not where I'm going.
WOMAN   Oh, I see. *(She doesn't)* Never? You must be going a long journey.
MAN   You could say that.
WOMAN   Could I ask ...?
MAN   No. Look, I think I've told you enough already.

Pause. The WOMAN is now a little out of her depth.

WOMAN   Well, that's certainly a new one. I've got no little box to tick for that! *(Laughs a little nervously)* Now, let's see - what's the next question? *(She looks)* Ah, yes. What do you think about identity cards? *(She lowers her clipboard)* Look, I don't mean to pry, but ...

MAN   Really? I thought that's exactly what you were doing. Is there much more? You did say 'only a minute.'
WOMAN   If you mean what I think you mean ... I'd like to help, that's all. Is there something I can do?
MAN   Nothing, no. Nothing at all. Now, if you'll excuse me.
WOMAN   *(Hurriedly)* No! You mustn't go. I mean *(Taps her clipboard)* the questions aren't over yet.
MAN   They are for me.
WOMAN   Just one or two more *(Pleads)* please?

MAN looks at his wristwatch.

You see, unless I'm mistaken ...

He waves his hand towards her clipboard.

MAN   The questions!

She returns reluctantly to her clipboard.

WOMAN   Do you think young people are marrying too early?
MAN   *(Decisively)* No.

She makes a note.

WOMAN   *(Confirms)* No. What do you think is the right time for marriage?
MAN   There isn't one. What's the right time for one person is not the right time for someone else. Marriage is right *when* it is right. And when its wrong - well, it doesn't matter what age you are. Believe me, I know.

She doesn't know what to make of this or what write down. He reacts to her confusion.

Look, perhaps you'd better ask somebody else.
WOMAN   *(Calmly)* You really *are* in trouble, aren't you?
MAN   Not now. *(Pause)* Now I've made up my mind.
WOMAN   Can you tell me about it?
MAN   Its too late. There's no point. And there's no turning back.
WOMAN   Can you tell me about it?

30.

MAN   You wouldn't understand.
WOMAN   I might.
MAN   *(Pause)* Those questions ... *(He points to her clipboard)* ... they tell you nothing.
WOMAN   *(Demurs)* Well ...
MAN   Nothing! Nothing important. Nobody *really* wants to know about people.
WOMAN   *(Earnestly)* Oh, I think you're wrong.
MAN   I could give you a list of questions - a short list - half a dozen, maybe. Simple questions that would shatter the peace of this precinct and throw people into a panic. Nothing like *(He mocks)* 'Have you get a video?' or 'Where do you go for your summer holidays?'
WOMAN   What questions?
MAN   You wouldn't be allowed to ask them. And I'll tell you something else - they wouldn't be answered.
WOMAN   You have to respect people's privacy.
MAN   *(Cynically)* Oh, yes, we all do *that*. And that's why *(He points)* this lady over here, and that man there may be screaming silently inside because of some problem no-one wants to know about. *(Subdued anger)* Or they are withering like a dried leaf because they can't remember when any one last showed them any real love. We must respect their privacy!

            Pause.

WOMAN   *(Quietly)* I said I would listen.

            Pause.

MAN   *(Shrugs)* There's no way forward for me.

            She returns his gaze steadily.

            (The anger has gone) My marriage was a failure. My job was a failure. Even my divorce was a failure. Now I've been laid off. The chance of getting work with my skills is remote. Oh yes - then there's my debt. Got all that?
WOMAN   And you feel all this makes you special?
MAN   At this point I don't feel anything.

31.

WOMAN	Do you know what I think? I think you are being very sorry for yourself.
MAN	You'll have to do better than that. I told myself that a long time ago. And I decided I had good reason to be sorry for myself. You've never felt like that?
WOMAN	Oh, yes - quite often. In fact that's just how I feel now.
MAN	*(Surprised)* You?
WOMAN	Your marriage failed. Mine never started.
MAN	*(Gently)* Go on.

Pause.

WOMAN	We were planning to be engaged when my mother became ill, and I had to nurse her.
MAN	*(Sympathetically)* Its an old story.
WOMAN	Yes. Oh, she was a wonderful mother. I didn't resent one day of it. *(Pause)* I nursed her for seven years before she died. *(Pause)* Of course, there was no engagement. I could hardly blame him.
MAN	And then?
WOMAN	My father was useless on his own.
MAN	*He* needed you.
WOMAN	Couldn't boil the proverbial egg. You men! I've looked after him for nine years. Now he's terminally ill. I do this job *(She waves her clipboard)* to get out occasionally and meet other people. I don't mind all that - but I can't bear to see him suffering.
MAN	I'm sorry.
WOMAN	Sometimes when he calls out to me I go to him and hold his hand - it breaks my heart. *(Pause)* I've even wondered - I've even wondered whether I should - well ...
MAN	Help him to ...?
WOMAN	No! *(Long pause)* Yes. Just to make it easier ... to ...
MAN	Easier to die?
WOMAN	Isn't it strange? I've never told this to anyone else.
MAN	But you wouldn't forgive yourself. You want to help your father lose his pain - but he would lose you too! You're all he's got. *(Gently)* Don't run away.
WOMAN	It seems so unfair.

MAN   Life *is* unfair. Isn't that the cliche? And its unfair to you.
           We have to cope with what we get. I guess there's going to
           be a lot of sorting out done somewhere - later on. Anyway
           ... *(He takes her hand)* ... you must hang on.
WOMAN   *(Grateful)* Thanks. *(Amazed)* But just now you ...
MAN   It's a bit odd, isn't it?
WOMAN   You were going to ...

           He releases her hand.

MAN   I know. *(Pause)* Perhaps you were sent.
WOMAN   No - you have helped *me*. Yet we don't know each other,
           do we? Perfect strangers.
MAN   Oh, I don't know. You know already that I have a TV and
           Video, but no dishwasher!

           *They both smile. Her smiles fades and she becomes
           concerned.*

WOMAN   What happens now - about you, I mean?
MAN   Good question. *(Pause)* Does it matter?
WOMAN   Of course it matters.
MAN   *(Serious and intrigued)* I really think you mean it.
WOMAN   *(She is embarrassed)* You could start by re-ordering your
           daily paper.
MAN   And *you* ?
WOMAN   *(Businesslike)* You haven't answered all my questions yet.

           *He looks admiringly at her, forcing her to look back
           quickly to her clipboard.*

MAN   You don't give up.
WOMAN   No. One last question. *(Looks at clipboard)* Do you attend
           any place of worship?
MAN   Sometimes, yes.

           She makes a note as he continues.

           St. Mary's in Maple Road.
WOMAN   *(She looks up, startled)* St Mary's! I go there too. How is
           it that we've never ...?

33.

MAN	Busy respecting everyone's privacy I expect! I sit on the right hand side.
WOMAN	I sit on the left!

They laugh.

MAN	I could ...
WOMAN	... easily change.

Short pause.

MAN	*(He offers his hand)* I'm Tim.
WOMAN	Jenny. *(She shakes his hand. They smile warmly at each other.)*
MAN	End of questions?
WOMAN	*(She nods, smiling)* End of questions.
MAN	*(He holds her gaze)* 'Bye, Jenny. *(Moves away)*
WOMAN	*(Calls)* Tim. *(He pauses)* You won't ...? I mean ...
MAN	The papers. I must cancel - the cancellation.
WOMAN	*(She smiles)* Shall I see you? Sunday perhaps?
MAN	Yes, I'd like that, Jenny. I'll be on the ... *(Waggles finger to indicate which side)*
WOMAN	*(Seriously)* I'll be on *your* side, Tim.

She holds his gaze for a long moment. He smiles and exits L.

Pause.

She continues to look L. for a moment, then becomes businesslike again. She sees someone offstage R. and begins to walk in that direction with her clipboard upraised.

Excuse me, madam, can you spare a minute ...?

She exits in pursuit of her next interview.

END

IN TOUCH

Characters: JACK and JEAN
                JOAN and GEORGE

JACK and JEAN meet centre stage. Arms are flung wide and they hug each other extravagantly, planting kisses on both cheeks (Mwuh! Mwuh!) in the current fashion. As they do so, JOAN and GEORGE come on together and meet the others, centre.

JACK   *(To JEAN)* Have you met each other? *(Indicating JOAN)*
JEAN   *(Brightly)* No. *(To JOAN)* Hallo. *(They hug and kiss warmly in the same fashion)*
JACK   George?
GEORGE Hallo.
JEAN   Hi! *(GEORGE and JEAN hug warmly)*
JACK   *(To JOAN and GEORGE)* So, what's new?
JOAN   I got that job I was after and I start tomorrow.
JACK   Great! *(JACK hugs JOAN. JEAN does the same.)*
GEORGE And guess what? We've managed to sell the flat.
JACK   Fantastic! *(JACK hugs GEORGE)*
JEAN   That's brilliant!   *(JEAN hugs GEORGE)*
JACK   Well, must go now.
JEAN   Great to meet up with you.

Everybody hugs everybody in turn. JACK and JEAN move off.

        'Bye. See you in Church.
GEORGE *(Apologetically)* Er ... afraid not. Sorry, we shan't be there.
JACK   *(Surprised)* Oh?
JOAN   We have a problem with the new minister.
JEAN   Really?
JOAN   Yes.
GEORGE He *insists* on the congregation 'passing the peace'.

JACK and JEAN smile. JOAN and GEORGE grimace. All move off L. and R.

END

35.

STAR STRUCK

Two women return from shopping at the supermarket laden with full carrier bags. They dump them down with relief.

A   Thank goodness for that. You'll stay for a coffee?

B   Yes, please. Just ready for it.

A   When that girl at the check-out said 'Would you like any cash back?' and I said 'I haven't given you any yet' she didn't laugh, did she? I was only joking. Black as usual?

B   Black, yes. You know, I've been thinking it'll soon be time to book our summer holiday.

A   I know. I've already got some brochures.

B   *(Surprised)* You didn't say.

A   I only picked them up yesterday. Just on an impulse.

B   You've got something up your sleeve, haven't you? Well, so have I. My Terry says it's time we all went somewhere different.

A   Like where?

B   Oh, I don't know. Haven't got that far yet. I've got a few ideas though.

A   Here's your coffee.

B   Thanks.

A   Well, let's hear it then.

B   It's only an idea. *(Pause)* I thought of Spain.

A   *(Horrified)* Spain!

B   Think of the sunshine. Guaranteed. You remember what Scarborough was like last year.

A   That was just unlucky. It's usually very nice. No, I can't say I want to go to Spain.

B   *(Disappointed)* Oh. All right then. How about this?

A   What?

B   Florida.

A   Florida!

B   It's a marvellous package. Not much dearer than Scarborough.

A   No, sorry, I'm not interested in Florida. That means we'd have to fly.

B   *(Gives up)* All right - where then? Where are your brochures for?

A produces a brochure and hands it to B.

B   *(Reads the title, aghast)* Norfolk Broads! On a boat? You're not serious? All the week on a boat? No, thank you. Whatever made you think of that? Supposing it got rough?

A   Rough? This is flat calm. It doesn't get rough on the Norfolk Broads.

B   *(Unconvinced)* H'm. What was your other idea?

A hands B a second brochure.

A   I suppose we can forget this too?

B   *(Reads)* 'A cruise to the Canaries'. Yes. *(B hands it back)*

A   Back to square one then.

B   Looks like it. When I said 'different' I didn't mean that different.

A   The truth is, I don't want to *fly*.

B   And I don't want to go on the *water*.

A   That's it then. It's back to Scarborough.

B   We've always enjoyed it.

A   I suppose so. We'll manage. It's only a week.

B   I'll tell Arthur that's its all been decided. *(They giggle mischievously)*

A   So - same as before then, the first week in July?

B   Right.

A   The fourth.

B   The fourth? No! Make it the eleventh.

A   It can't be the eleventh.

B   But Harry only gets two weeks, it's got to be one or the other.

A   Well, it just can't be the eleventh.

B   And it definitely can't be the fourth.

A   That's it, then. We can't go. Not together.

B   But we've *always* gone together. Are you sure you can't change?

A   Absolutely. What about you?

B   No way. Well, I'd better be going. We'll have to think about all this.

A   Yes, perhaps when you've thought about it and talked to Harry you can come up with something.

B   Or perhaps *you* could.

A	I don't think so. You see, well, I've been warned.
B	What do you mean?
A	I've been warned.
B	About what?
A	For a start I've been warned not to fly. So that's Florida out.
B	Oh, I see.
A	And my unlucky number is eleven. So I can't travel on the eleventh.
B	Well *I've* been warned as well.
A	Have you?
B	I mustn't go over the water, and my unlucky number is four. So no Norfolk Broads, and I couldn't travel on the fourth. You see I'm a Capricorn.
A	So am I.
B	But ...!
A	How can we have the same star sign ...?
B	... and be told such different things?
A	I read mine in the Family Life Magazine.
B	And I read mine in the Daily Echo.
A	They can't both be right.
B	So.
A	They're both probably ...
BOTH	Wrong!

The phone rings.

A	I'll get it. *(Pause)* Hallo. Oh, hallo Harry. *(To B)* It's for you. *(She hands the phone over to B)*
B	Hallo, Harry. Yes as a matter of fact we *have* been talking about it. What do you mean we can *stop* talking about it? Oh you have, have you? *(B covers the mouthpiece and talks to A)* He says don't make any plans because he's already booked the holiday. *(B returns to listening to the phone)* You've what! That sounds marvellous. Is that from Heathrow? *(Listens)*

B speaks to A.

B	To Miami !

B listens to phone again.

B	Then by boat to the Caribbean. Sounds wonderful. No we haven't tied anything up. So we travel on the fourth and travel back on the eleventh? That's fine. No problem. Bye, dear.
A	That settles that. Thank goodness he's had no 'warning' like us. Not interested in star signs I suppose.
B	Oh, but he is. He's worse than me.
A	And what star sign is he?
B	Capricorn.
A	Capricorn! Well what about the water, and flying?
B	No problem. He takes the Evening Chronicle.

END

'The voice that rolls the stars along speaks all the promises.'
Isaac Watts

CALLED TO PREACH

Characters: CHURCH STEWARD
              MAN

A Steward prepares for morning service in the Vestry. A man carrying a Bible enters. He looks very worried.

STEWARD 'Morning. Come in. You haven't left yourself much time.
MAN   Excuse me, this is the vestry? I was sent to the vestry.
S'WARD   That's right. You haven't been here before, have you?
MAN   No, not in here.
S'WARD   You'll soon find your way round. The folk here are very friendly.
MAN   About my car. You see ...
S'WARD   That's no problem. Leave it to me. Now - would you like *me* to read the Notices?
MAN   Notices? Oh, I see ... no, no, you don't understand ...
S'WARD   Its all right. I'm not offended. Some prefer to do it themselves, some don't. It's all the same to me.
MAN   All I wanted to say was ...

Steward looks at his watch.

S'WARD   We're a bit pressed for time. Shall we have a word of prayer?
MAN   *(Alarmed)* Prayer? No, there's no need for that.
S'WARD   No need? Can't agree with you there. You need it, I need it, we all need it.
MAN   Oh, dear. No, listen - it's about my car. You see ...
S'WARD   *(Surprised)* You want me to pray about the car? Aren't you worrying too much about it? Just leave it to me. Now - remember to speak up, and if you don't go too much over the hour they're sure to invite you again.

The MAN does not smile.

S'WARD   Just my little joke.
MAN   But I'm no preacher!

S'WARD   Very few of them are, believe me. Now - you'll find a glass of water in the pulpit and the book's already open at the first hymn. Is there anything else?

MAN   I'm just an ordinary chap like *(Points to door)* all them in the congregation.

S'WARD   I *like* your attitude. Can't stand the pompous ones who think they are God's gift to us. There's a good crowd this morning. Are you ready, then?

MAN   Ready? *(Horrified)* I'm not going in there!!

S'WARD   Not going? Come, come. You *are* worked up, aren't you?

MAN   You don't seem to realise ...

S'WARD   Here, have one of these. I take them for my ulcer - it'll calm you down. *(Offers a tablet)*

MAN   No thanks. I *am* calm. And I'm *not* going in there!

S'WARD   It's good to have nerves just before going on, so they say.

MAN   *(Patiently)* Let me try again. About my car ...

S'WARD   You're obsessed about that car, aren't you? It's taken you over - 'tisn't healthy, you know. Just what *is* the problem? You've got thirty seconds to tell me.

MAN   The problem is - I've rammed my car into a Rover 400 in your car park and caused quite a lot of damage. The occupant of the Rover has been taken off to hospital.

S'WARD   Oh, dear. I *am* sorry. You should have said. *(Pause)* But you mustn't let that put you off preaching.

MAN   *(Hysterical)* But I am *not* the preacher! The man in the Rover was the preacher.

S'WARD   *(Pause)* Ah! That *does* make a difference. I'll have to mention that in the Notices. *(Writes a note)* Come on then, its past time. *(Goes to door)* Don't drink the water, it's last week's. And watch those four steps into the pulpit. *(Pushes the man through the door and calls after him)* Every blessing. We're all with you.

STEWARD exits with Notices book and collection plate, shaking his head.

END

41.

CAUGHT IN THE NET

Characters: BILL   Husband
                    BET   Wife

BILL is sitting at a computer. The screen could be angled to be seen or not as desired. A mug of tea is on the table close to the computer. BET, his wife, is standing at an ironing board. There is a large pile of ironing waiting to be done. As she irons she holds up a small child's dress. BILL clatters away the keyboard, looking up frequently at the screen.

BILL   There he is! It's unbelievable. I feel I already know this chap. *(Pause)* The other side of the world.

                    Pause.

BET   Your tea's going cold.
BILL   *(Looking at the screen)* He's says he's sitting there in this big bungalow - blazing log fire and everything.
BET   Who is?
BILL   Emile. At a place called Churchill in Northern Canada. He says its freezing.
BET   D'you want that tea or not?
BILL   Eh? *(Realises)* Oh. *(He sips the tea not taking his eyes off the screen, quickly putting the mug down.)* Uggh! It's stone cold. *(With awe)* Sitting here, Bet I'm in touch with the world. Anywhere. Youngsters are all into this now. Just think - when they are old they'll never feel cut off, they'll have friends all over the world. Never be lonely - they'll just go surfing. Isn't that something? *(Pause)* Sounds like the baby crying. *(Still looking at screen)* It's all right, I'll go.

He doesn't. After a moment, BET exits. BILL carries on 'surfing'. BET returns and continues ironing. BILL speaks, not looking up.

Is she O.K?

BET goes to answer ...

Hang on. Who's this? It's a bloke from Florida. He's into collecting old war stuff. Looking for old posters - you know 'Your country needs you' or 'Coughs and sneezes spread diseases.' 'Be like Dad, keep Mum.' Can I smell something burning, Bet? *(Sniffs)* It's that cake.

BET exits. BILL continues, absorbed. In her absence he reads out loud what he is typing.

'Hello, Jeff, I haven't any posters but I do have a collection of medals from WW2. I think one of them might be rare. Are you interested?'

BET returns and continues ironing. BILL speaks to BET while peering at the screen.

Your Dad didn't get his medals out much did he? Just lying in that draw. There's a chap here who's dead keen. Seems to want anything like that.

The phone rings.

I'll get it. *(Still typing)* Just a minute. Coming. *(Types on)*

BET exits. The phone stops ringing. BET returns. BILL still screen watching.

	Who was it? Anybody?
BET	Nobody.
BILL	Good! *(Pause)* There's a woman here from Oslo. Isn't this unbelievable? Oslo. I just feel my life is sort of expanding. We live on a big map, Bet. All the world in our room. What's this? *(He peers harder at the screen)* She says - this woman - that she has the secret of a happy marriage. *(Cynically)* Oh, yes?
BET	Well she's not the only one.
BILL	*(Not looking up)* Did you say something, dear?
BET	*(Wearily with heavy emphasis)* I said ...
BILL	*(Still not hearing)* What?
BET	I said she's not the only ... *(Exasperated)* Oh!

She gives up and goes over to him, turns his shoulders and plants a kiss on his lips. She returns to her ironing. Unfazed, BILL turns back to the screen instantly absorbed again.

BILL   *(Pause)* What was all that about?

He continues typing. BET puts on a pair of earphones and switches on a personal stereo. She resumes ironing. BILL looks round, then back to the screen.

I don't think you've heard a word I said.

END